OCEAN LIFE UP CLOSE

seals

by Rebecca Pettiford

BLASTOFF! READERS 3

BELLWETHER MEDIA • MINNEAPOLIS, MN

Note to Librarians, Teachers, and Parents:

Blastoff! Readers are carefully developed by literacy experts and combine standards-based content with developmentally appropriate text.

Level 1 provides the most support through repetition of high-frequency words, light text, predictable sentence patterns, and strong visual support.

Level 2 offers early readers a bit more challenge through varied simple sentences, increased text load, and less repetition of high-frequency words.

Level 3 advances early-fluent readers toward fluency through increased text and concept load, less reliance on visuals, longer sentences, and more literary language.

Level 4 builds reading stamina by providing more text per page, increased use of punctuation, greater variation in sentence patterns, and increasingly challenging vocabulary.

Level 5 encourages children to move from "learning to read" to "reading to learn" by providing even more text, varied writing styles, and less familiar topics.

Whichever book is right for your reader, Blastoff! Readers are the perfect books to build confidence and encourage a love of reading that will last a lifetime!

This edition first published in 2017 by Bellwether Media, Inc.

No part of this publication may be reproduced in whole or in part without written permission of the publisher. For information regarding permission, write to Bellwether Media, Inc., Attention: Permissions Department, 5357 Penn Avenue South, Minneapolis, MN 55419.

Library of Congress Cataloging-in-Publication Data

Names: Pettiford, Rebecca, author.
Title: Seals / by Rebecca Pettiford.
Description: Minneapolis, MN : Bellwether Media, Inc., 2017. | Series: Blastoff! Readers. Ocean Life Up Close | Includes bibliographical references and index. | Audience: Ages 5 to 8. | Audience: Grades K to 3.
Identifiers: LCCN 2016034480 (print) | LCCN 2016042928 (ebook) | ISBN 9781626175747 (hardcover : alk. paper) | ISBN 9781681032955 (ebook)
Subjects: LCSH: Seals (Animals)–Juvenile literature.
Classification: LCC QL737.P6 P48 2017 (print) | LCC QL737.P6 (ebook) | DDC 599.79–dc23
LC record available at https://lccn.loc.gov/2016034480

Text copyright © 2017 by Bellwether Media, Inc. BLASTOFF! READERS and associated logos are trademarks and/or registered trademarks of Bellwether Media, Inc. SCHOLASTIC, CHILDREN'S PRESS, and associated logos are trademarks and/or registered trademarks of Scholastic Inc.

Editor: Christina Leighton   Designer: Brittany McIntosh

Printed in the United States of America, North Mankato, MN.

Table of Contents

What Are Seals?	4
On the Move	12
Sharp Swimmers	16
Seal Pups	20
Glossary	22
To Learn More	23
Index	24

What Are Seals?

Seals are ocean **mammals** with long, round bodies. Their **blubber** keeps them warm.

Other Pinnipeds

fur seals

sea lions

walruses

front flipper

These **pinnipeds** have two **flippers** in front. They have two larger flippers in back.

There are many types of seals. Harp seals and most others live in the cold waters of the **Arctic** or **Antarctic**.

Hawaiian monk seal

Species Spotlight
HARBOR SEAL

life span: 30 years

depth range: 0 to 1,575 feet (0 to 480 meters)

harbor seal range = ▭

conservation status: least concern

Extinct | Extinct in the Wild | Critically Endangered | Endangered | Vulnerable | Near Threatened | Least Concern

Some live in warmer waters, like Hawaiian monk seals. Baikal seals live only in **freshwater**!

Seals have whiskers and small heads. These mammals have ear holes that close when they dive.

Identify a Seal

blubber — ear holes — whiskers

Their short hair is light or dark. Some seals also have spots.

southern elephant seal

ringed seal

The ringed seal is the smallest. It weighs up to 150 pounds (68 kilograms).

The southern elephant seal is the largest. It can weigh up to 8,800 pounds (3,992 kilograms)!

Seal Sizes

Smallest
ringed seal

average human

up to 5 feet
(1.5 meters) long

Largest
southern elephant seal

average human

up to 20 feet
(6 meters) long

On the Move

Seals swim by moving their rear flippers back and forth. They use their front flippers to turn.

Mediterranean monk seal

On land, seals pull themselves forward with their front flippers. They wiggle up and down on their bellies.

Seals go on land to rest, get warm, and have **pups**. Once a year, they also gather on land to **molt**.

Like many mammals, seals need to shed their old hair and skin. Molting takes about four weeks.

Sharp Swimmers

Seals cannot swim faster than most **predators**, but they can turn quickly. They can even swim upside down!

They must watch out for hungry sharks, orcas, and polar bears.

Sea Enemies

great white sharks

orcas

polar bears

Catch of the Day

 Antarctic krill

 Pacific herring

 common octopus

Seals are **carnivores**. These hunters dive to find krill, octopuses, and fish.

They swallow food whole or tear off chunks with their sharp teeth. Harbor seals eat up to 18 pounds (8 kilograms) each day!

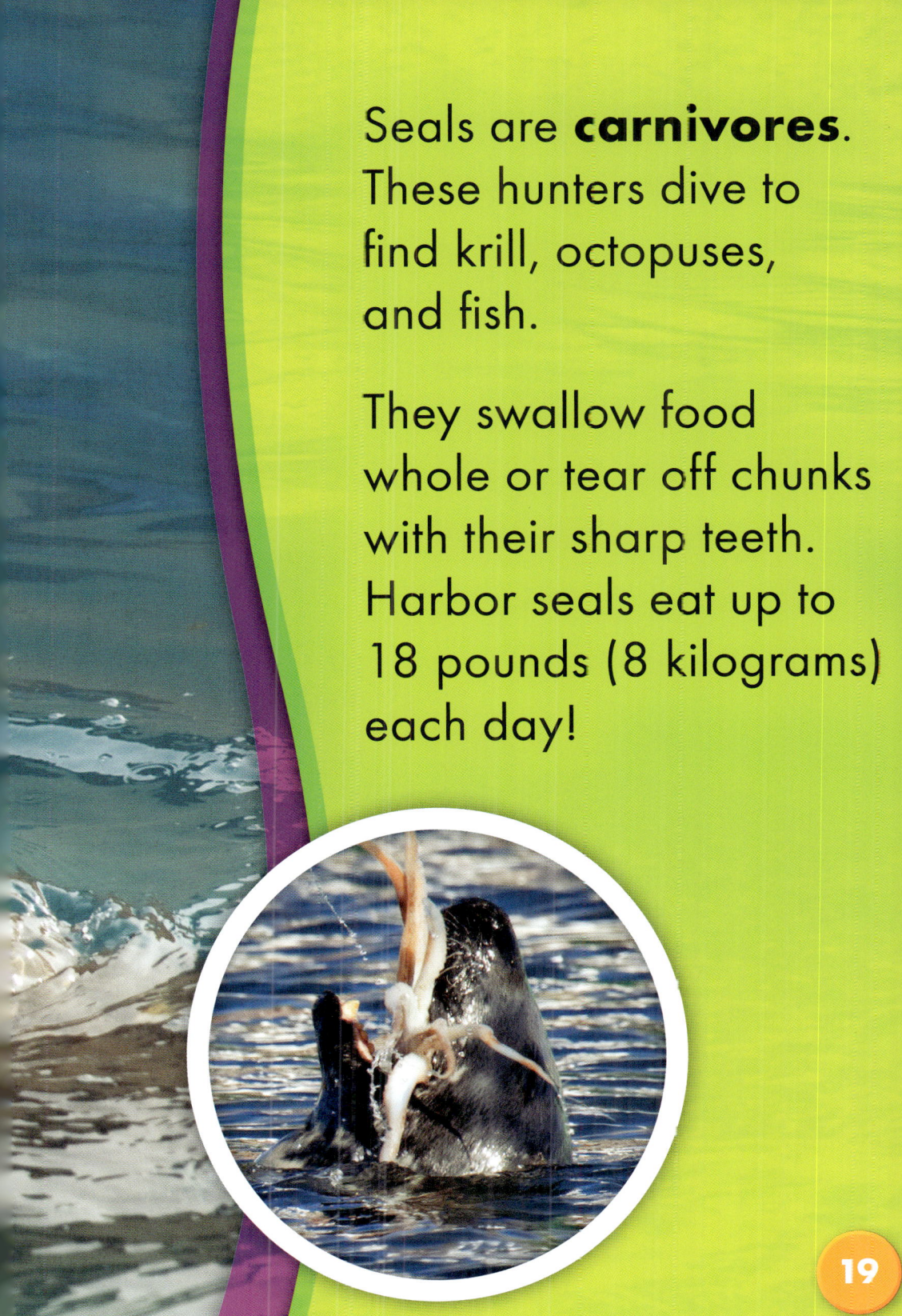

Seal Pups

Once a year, a mother seal has one pup. The pup drinks its mother's milk.

harp seals

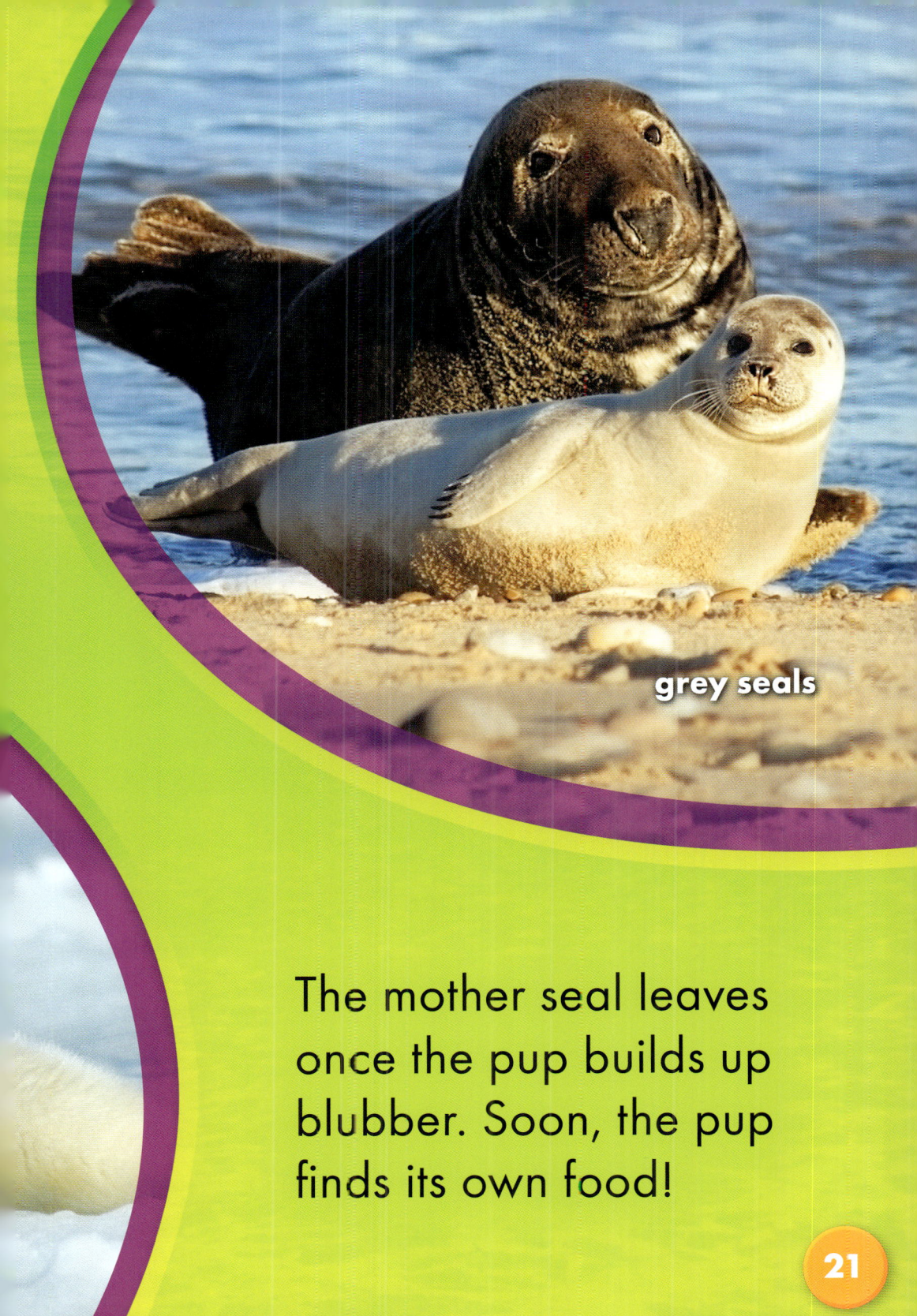

grey seals

The mother seal leaves once the pup builds up blubber. Soon, the pup finds its own food!

Glossary

Antarctic—the cold region around the South Pole

Arctic—the cold region around the North Pole

blubber—the fat of seals

carnivores—animals that only eat meat

flippers—flat, wide body parts that are used for swimming

freshwater—water that is not salty

mammals—warm-blooded animals that have backbones and feed their young milk

molt—to shed fur so a new layer can grow

pinnipeds—ocean mammals with four flippers; seals, sea lions, and walruses are pinnipeds.

predators—animals that hunt other animals for food

pups—baby seals

To Learn More

AT THE LIBRARY
King, Zelda. *Seals*. New York, N.Y.: PowerKids Press, 2012.

Ryndak, Rob. *Seal or Sea Lion?* New York, N.Y.: Gareth Stevens Publishing, 2016.

Spilsbury, Louise. *Seal*. Chicago, Ill.: Heinemann Library, 2011.

ON THE WEB
Learning more about seals is as easy as 1, 2, 3.

1. Go to www.factsurfer.com.

2. Enter "seals" into the search box.

3. Click the "Surf" button and you will see a list of related web sites.

With factsurfer.com, finding more information is just a click away.

Index

Antarctic, 6
Arctic, 6
bellies, 13
blubber, 4, 8, 21
bodies, 4
carnivores, 19
depth, 7
dive, 8, 19
ear holes, 8
eat, 19
flippers, 5, 12, 13
food, 18, 19, 21
hair, 9, 15
heads, 8
land, 13, 14
life span, 7
mammals, 4, 8, 15
molt, 14, 15
pinnipeds, 5
predators, 16, 17
pups, 14, 20, 21
range, 6, 7
size, 10, 11
skin, 15
spots, 9
status, 7
swim, 12, 16
teeth, 19
types, 6
whiskers, 8

The images in this book are reproduced through the courtesy of: George Karbus Photography/ Glow Images, front cover; Robert HM Voors, p. 3; Minden Pictures/ SuperStock, pp. 4-5; SkyLynx, p. 5 (top); Longjourneys, p. 5 (center); Vladimir Melnik, p. 5 (bottom); NatPar Collection/ Alamy, p. 6; Devin_Taylor-Photography, p. 7; Volodymyr Goinyk, p. 8 (top left); bierchen, p. 8 (top center); Petr Rerucha, p. 8 (top right); Eric Isselee, p. 8 (bottom); Andrea Leone, p. 9; David Osborn, p. 10 (top); CORDIER Sylvain/ Hemis.fr/ SuperStock, p. 10 (bottom); zaferkizilkaya, p. 12; Sergey Tarasenko, p. 13; Trudy Simmons, p. 14; Amelie Koch, p. 15; VisionDive, p. 17 (top left); Andrea Izzotti, p. 17 (top center); Iakov Filimonov, p. 17 (top right); Juniors Bildarchiv GmbH/ Alamy, p. 17 (bottom); Dmytro Pylypenko, p. 18 (top left); Daiju Azuma/ Wikipedia, p. 18 (top center); magnusdeepbelow, p. 18 (top right); Tim Burrett, p. 18 (bottom); MarkMowbray, p. 19; Stone Nature Photography/ Alamy, p. 20; Richard Bowden, p. 21.